© Uzochukwu Mike 2019

Published by:

Smart Connect

No 2 Lucas Road, Abraka

Delta state

Nigeria

All rights reserved. No part of this publication may be reproduced, stored in a retrieval system, or transmitted in any form or by any means, electronic, mechanical, photocopying, recording, or otherwise, without the prior written permission of the author.

DEDICATION

This book is dedicated to my parents, Mr and Mrs Okechukwu Okwuagbala. You are one of the best parents on the planet earth.

ACKNOWLEDGEMENTS

To Mercy Okwuagbala

I decided to acknowledge you first because you are a great mother. Without you mom, I would not have been a graduate from university. When it became tough, I thought I could not complete my first degree. As a good mother, you never allowed that happen. You picked it upon yourself to make effort and made my university education successful to the end. I sincerely appreciate your support even after my university days. During my training under FBN Insurance and College of Insurance and Financial Management of Nigeria, you still showed concern. Thank you so much mom.

To Izunwanne Chinwe Dorothy

Even as a mother of two when I was still a student in the university, you did not give up on me. You are a great sister Chinwe. You are courageous and empowering sister. Thanks so much for many positive imparts you made in my life.

To Nnaji Anayochukwu Kenneth and Chanomi Merit

I decided to acknowledge you two, Kenneth and Merit because you two are powerful policyholders. I am your financial advisors and you have been good at taking my advice. I also want to appreciate you Chanomi Merit for the referrals you have given to me in insurance business.

To Ekhator Godwin

I want to use this opportunity to appreciate my own unit manager Ekhator Godwin for pushing me to the level I am today as a financial advisor in FBN Insurance. You made sales so easy and something to love for all the financial advisors under you. A man that always makes his people understands that where they are today is better than where they were yesterday.

To FBN Insurance Abraka Unit

You are a formidable team of financial advisors. Sometimes we gist, we smile and we make one another angry in the office. But that is what makes us people with different characters. Thank you all for your tips and ideas. More importantly, I want to appreciate my own personal persons Nwaeke Gideon, Eiythan Stanley, and Okere Ese.

TABLE OF CONTENTS

DEDICATION………………………………………………….ii

ACKNOWLEDGEMENTS………………………………..iii

TABLE OF CONTENTS……………………………….....v

Chapter 1…………………………………………………1

Introduction to Insurance Prospects and Customers

References

Chapter 2………………………………………………….9

Terms used in Insurance

References

Chapter 3………………………………………………...22

Sum Assured

3.1 Factors Affecting Sum Assured

3.2 Recalculation of Sum Assured

3.3 The use of Sum Assured in Policies

References

Chapter 4………………………………………………...38

Insincerity among Insurance Agents

4.1 Why do some Insurance Agents lie a lot?

References

Chapter 5………………………………………………..46

Buying Insurance Policies and Signing Terms and Conditions

5.1 Why you should Read Insurance Policies Terms and Conditions (T & C)…

References

Chapter 6..54

Insurance Policies and Interest

6.1 Underpayment can be experienced

6.2 Choosing to Pay Higher Premium

References

Chapter 7..62

Insurance Product Design

7.1 Examples of Different Product Designs

7.2 Comparing Design Benefits

7.3 Buying Insurance from Different Companies due to Design

References

Chapter 8..71

Agents Attitude towards Policy Termination

8.1 Policy Termination and Agent Demotion

8.2 Termination and Loss of Earnings

8.3 Unfair Treatment during Termination

References

Chapter 9..78

Term Insurance

9.1 What is Term Insurance?

9.2 Who can Buy Term Insurance?

9.3 Conditions for making Claim in Term Insurance

References

Chapter 10..**86**

The Importance of Buying Insurance

10.1 Importance of General Insurance

10.2 The Importance of Life Insurance

10.3 The Importance of Insurance to Nations

References

Chapter 11...**95**

Claim Making

11.1 Insurance Companies pay Claim

11.2 Facts on Claims Paid by Insurance Industry

11.3 You are paid at the due Date

11.4 Go for Your Claim at the Right Time

11.5 Requirements to make Claim

References

Other Books by the Author.................................**115**

Chapter 1

Introduction to Insurance Prospects and Customers

There are young men and women who are on the streets and offices searching for customers. These people dress well and appear smart in their dealing. Their tongues are sugar-coated and they sweet talk prospects to buy what they sell. They do not market or advertise bank accounts opening. They sell policies to people. These men and women are called insurance agents, sales persons or financial advisors.

They sell insurance services to many people to increase in their earnings. Good insurance agents always check on their prospects and customers, encouraging them to pay their premiums for the insurance plans they have entered. These agents appear kind and caring as they encourage their customers to keep paying their premiums. It is not as if they just do this because they are kind people but they do such things because they want to be earning their own commissions at the due time.

The truth is, the moment a customer that a financial advisor brought into an insurance company stops paying, the agent stops earning from such customer. For any money paid by a policyholder, the agent that manages the policy earns commission on it. So, when they show some care, just know that they do not show such concern in vein. They target something. No insurance agent is happy seeing his customer not paying his or her premiums.

They can use the last money in their hands to attend your occasions. They do these because they want to maintain relationship with you. A good insurance agent makes sure he attends the occasions of their customers.

There are some terms that a customer to an insurance company may not understand. These terminologies sometimes appear foreign to customers and prospects. But it is understandable because insurance is not the area of many prospects and customers. Examples of such terms are premium, sum assured, cooling off period, waiting period and the rest. Explanation on some of these terms will be given in the later chapter.

An insurance company may not tell you all you need to know before you sign for any insurance contract. That is the reason you need to understand insurance before going into it fully. It is not all about sign here and sign here and you do that as fast as possible as directed by the agent. Take your time and go through the form before signing anytime. It is not as if insurance is a bad thing to sign into but you have to understand some clauses first.

On entering into any insurance plan, there are some things you have to understand. One of the things is "no premium no cover" aspect. If a policyholder in any insurance company do not pay his premiums after some time, he is likely to lose some of the benefits covered by the policy. There is always duration a policy can stay and lapse. It is not all about what a salesperson told you because he wants to make sales but the fact that applies in every insurance policy.

When a policyholder do not pay the premium he or she is expected to pay from the beginning, there can be recalculation of the sum assured. Do not be worried about the term "sum assured" as more will be highlighted on the term later. Premium payment as when due is important so insurance customers should take that into consideration.

Do not be surprised to hear that some insurance agents are "technical liars". Some may not tell you all the truth you need to know about some policies. There are reasons behind this attitude of many agents that hunt for customers' every day. But, we will discuss more on this attitude of many agents and why they do what they do.

Insurance plans or services are not designed for interest purpose. If you are buying any insurance policy, be the product life or none life product, do not build your hopes around the interest you will gain at the end of the policy maturity. In life insurance products, there are investment policies that are designed over the years. These investment products which are insurance products are brought into market to help people save for some time. During the period of investing, the policyholders are not allowed to have access to the money until maturity date is reached.

Many pick these plans with the eyes of receiving interests at the end of the investment. No insurance plan is designed fundamentally for the purpose of you to get huge interest at the end. Such investment products are created for saving purpose and not for interest.

But in term insurance, a policyholder can have higher sum assured. But for the huge money to be paid, the policyholder must first of all die. In the other words, the beneficiary receives this huge amount of money which we can indirectly say has good interest rate. But here, the holder of the policy is not there to enjoy the money with the family members.

So at this point, disregard any big interest rate an agent gave you that you will get at the end of the savings in endowment plan. It is just a "format" for him or her to make sales. Insurance is not a ponzi scheme where you make a lot of interest by saving with the policy designed by any insurance company. Insurance companies are made of businessmen and women so do not expect them to give you all the profits they make as interest because you have a policy with them.

Instead of looking for interest by saving with insurance company of your choice as a policyholder, make sure you pay your premiums as you suppose to do pay. Some pick insurance policies to save towards their retirement as civil servants and expecting good return from insurance companies they invest in but end up disappointed. Some are underpaid at the end instead of having interest added to them. There are some factors that determine how much claim a policyholder takes home. For investment policies in insurance, the factors are age of the policyholder at the commencement of the policy, the duration chosen, method of payment and the premium paid.

Insurance products are not designed the same way. The way "company A" designs their own insurance product may not be same way "Company B" designs her own product. The design approach varies. The company a particular policyholder has a policy with may not allow him to see better design in another company's insurance product because they do not want to lose such customer to another company.

There are many insurance companies outside there with different design in their products. "Company A" may charge her policyholder that wants to surrender his policy at the fourth year but may not be same with the design of same kind of product being offered by "Company B". In "company B", you can surrender the policy at the second year without charge from your total paid premium.

In the recent years, insurance companies have taken different direction on how they do their businesses. Insurers today have embraced better innovative approaches that have not been in existence before. This includes flexibility in their insurance services, design of apps that customers can use to track their activities, and improvement in their consumer relationship. So do not see the insurance your grandfather bought in 1960 as the same as what applies today in 2019. A lot of positive changes have occurred.

Insurers are stuck in the past, doing business in a way that alienates their customers. Products are often rigid and inflexible. For example, when a customer wants an automobile insurance policy, they have to pay for coverage even when a vehicle sits idle at work or at home. People only drive maybe 3 to 5 percent of the day, and yet they're charged for having 24/7 coverage. The product doesn't actually fit their needs (Shoshana Weizenblut 2017). There is competition in the market and no insurance company wants to lose.

We come across risk every day. And for us not to be hit hard and feel bad when it occurs, the need for insurance coverage arises. There are benefits attached to insurance. Customers should see these benefits and buy insurance services for risk management approach. More on the good sides of choosing insurance services or products will be discussed as a separate chapter. Insurance benefits individuals, organizations and society in more ways than the average person realizes. Some of the benefits of insurance are obvious while others are not (CAFON 2018).

The main aim of buying insurance is to protect the insured of risk or the unforeseen but the joy in it is to make claim without much stress. Some insurance companies may not call you for claim so you have to be at alert always. When it is time for consumers to make their claim, they are to meet their agents or the insurer. Claim gives joy to the policyholders and the beneficiaries.

But, there are requirements to make claim. First of all you have your policy number. As policy number is to insurance, account number is to banking. Policy number given to you is a tracking number given to your policy alone. It is through this policy number that the payments made by policyholders are tracked. It is through it that all the payments made by the policyholder show. In the other words, once the policy number of a particular insurance holder is typed in the statement section in the computer used by the administrator and the enter button hit, it displays all the premiums paid by the insured.

We are going to do justice to the requirements needed before claim is paid to the policyholder or the beneficiary depending on the type of insurance policy. For instance, the approach to make claim in education insurance is different from that of auto insurance. An auto insurance claim is a request made to an insurance company for compensation for damages sustained after a car accident, or for representation or intervention on the insured's behalf when they are liable for damages (Mila Araujo 2019). Claim is an important area when it comes to insurance and therefore will be treated in detail.

References

- CAFON (2018), The Benefits of Insurance to Individuals, Organizations and Society, published by Consumer Advocacy Foundation of Nigeria, Ikeja, Lagos State, Nigeria
- Mila Araujo (2019), How to File an Auto Insurance Claim, published by The Balance, New York, United States
- Shoshana Weizenblut (2017), The Insurance Industry's Next Big Hurdle: Customer Centricity, published by Business.com, Waltham, MA, United States

Chapter 2

Terms used in Insurance

There are many terms used by insurance experts in their day to day insurance businesses. As a prospect or customer to any insurance company, it is important you know about these terms. These terms will help you understand some things whenever you are purchasing any insurance. Also, it will help you know when an agent wants to play you because he wants to make sales. Some agents may not explain these terms to you so you do not change your mind to not buying insurance from them again. So, know these terms and add to your knowledge.

Here, we will be looking at the terms used in insurance all over the world. These are terms used in everyday businesses in the world of risk management. Every insurance customer or prospect has to be conversant with these terms for easy communication.

Marketing

Marketing is the process of determining consumer demand for a product or service, motivating its sales, and distributing it into ultimate consumption at a profit. According to Nwaiwu, marketing is a set of activities that facilitate exchange transactions involving economic goods and services for the ultimate purpose of satisfying human need. In marketing, insurance agents talk to prospects persuading them to pick one or two products to satisfy the needs of the prospect. The positive end product of marketing is closing of the business or simply put as production. Production is the expected fruit of marketing.

Premium

Premium is the money paid by a policy holder to keep the insurance contract he or she entered always active. According to Julia Kagan, an insurance premium is the amount of money that an individual or business must pay for an insurance policy (Julia 2019). When there is no payment of premium as of when due, the insured will lose his or her cover. Premium can be paid monthly, quarterly, half yearly, annually or as lump sum (also called single premium).

Sum assured

Sum assured is the total guaranteed amount of money a policyholder will claim at the maturity of the policy so far the initial agreed premiums are paid as suppose. The sum assured is the amount of money an insurance policy guarantees to pay up before any bonuses are added. In other words, sum assured is the guaranteed amount the policyholder will receive. Sum assured is calculated at the initial signing in to any insurance policy. If there is increase in premium as contrary to the agreed sum at the commencement of the policy, the sum assured can be recalculated. Also, if the customer defaults in paying of premiums as of when due, the sum assured can be reduced at the maturity of the policy.

Suspect

A suspect in insurance is a potential prospect. When an insurance agent sees an individual first and thinks that the person can register into any insurance product, the person becomes a suspect. This is before meeting the person. The agent suspects that the individual or the organization can enter into any of the products he sells. Please know that suspect is different from prospect. It is suspect that transforms to prospect.

Prospect

From suspect to prospect. A prospect is a potential new customer who is approached and persuaded to buy an insurance policy. When an agent approaches an individual and begins to talk to the person to buy one or two insurance policies for himself or any other person, the person being spoken to at that point becomes a prospect. The agent may choose to market all the life products they have in their company and at the end they exchanged phone numbers. The exchange of the contacts is for the final closing of the business. But not all prospects end up being policyholders. Some prospects end up not buying maybe because of financial challenges, lost of interest or any other factor.

Customer

A customer is someone who registers a policy in any insurance company. But a customer can still be an organization. Example is when Harvard University registers a policy that will cover all the staff of the school against death. A customer is a prospect who enters into contract with an insurance company by having any of the plans designed by the company.

Policyholder

A policyholder is the same as a customer. But, policyholder is mostly used in insurance generally. He is a person or organization to whom an insurance policy is issued. In the other words, a policyholder is a person or organization that is insured by an insurance company to help manage any particular risk. As account holders are to bank so are policyholders to insurance. Active policyholders are the strength of insurance companies.

Insured

An insured is any individual or group whose life is covered by an insurance company. The person who obtains or is otherwise covered by insurance on his or her health, life, or property is an insured. He is the person who transfers a risk to an insurance company to stay safe in case of a contingent or uncertain loss. According to Prem Jhamnani of Insurance Institute of India, an insured is a person who is the buyer of the insurance policy (Prem Jhamnani 2018). Customer, policyholder and the insured are used interchangeably in insurance. But a policyholder is not always the insured. Example, a man can pick a general insurance policy in an insurance company to insure the home where he lives and the properties. In this case, the insured is the home and the properties.

Insurer

An entity which provides insurance is known as an insurer, insurance company, insurance carrier or underwriter. An Insurer is a company who sells insurance policies. Insurer is the one who bears the risk in return for consideration which is known as premium (Prem Jhamnani 2018). Examples of insurers are FBN Insurance, LeadWay Insurance, Sanlam Group Insurance Company of South Africa, Securian Financial (Minnesota Life Insurance Company), John Hancock Life Insurance of United States, Haven Life of United States, and ICICI Prudential Life Insurance of India. These and many others are insurers.

Beneficiary

A beneficiary is the person that benefits from an insurance policy. There is primary and secondary beneficiary. The primary beneficiary is the person (or persons) who will receive the proceeds of the life insurance policy when the insured person dies (Trusted Choice 2013). Secondary beneficiary is an assistant who takes the claim in the absence of the primary. When entering into insurance contract, the policyholder can choose to have more than one beneficiary which is in other words beneficiaries. A beneficiary is the person a claim is paid to in the event of death of the policy holder. But in a situation where the beneficiary is a minor as appears in some educational policies, the claim is paid to the guardian to the beneficiary who can be a second beneficiary as well.

DDM form

The acronym DDM stands for direct debit mandate. DDM form in that regard stands for direct debit mandate form. It is a form that a policyholder/insured filled for the insurance company to be making debit from his/her bank account for payment of premium. The debit from the policyholder's bank account can take place on monthly basis, quarterly, half yearly or yearly depending on the choice of the customer. Some customers fill DDM form for easy payment of their premiums and to maintain consistency in their premium payment. Why policyholders fill the form, it saves them the stress of going to the insurance company or banks to make their payment in the insurance company's account (s). With DDM form, payment is programmed and done automatically at the date filled by the policyholder for the debit to be made from his or her account.

Proposal form

The term proposal form is the form filled by the insured to enter into insurance contract with the insurer. Note that insurer as used here can be an insurance company. A proposal form is the form completed by the policyholder when applying for insurance (123 Money Ltd 2014). Once someone signs a proposal form, makes his premium payment into the account of the insurance company he signed the contract with, the person becomes a policyholder. When purchasing insurance, it is necessary for the prospect to provide the insurer with information so that it can assess the risk. This is usually done by filling in a proposal form, often available from agents, brokers, or insurers (Isaac Ng'aru 2014).

Termination

It is the ending of a policy before its due time. It is a general term used to refer to the end of coverage under a certain policy, usually due to the policy's term ending or due to cancellation. In life insurance, this term refers to the end of coverage of a policy due to the insured no longer paying the premiums. Some policyholders terminate their life policies when they are faced with challenges and in return needs the money they have saved with the insurance company.

Know that insurance is not all about claim at death. Insurance have savings, investment, or endowment plans that people (policyholders) save their money with as well. Termination is made before maturity of any policy. Depending on the way any insurance company design their policies, the policyholders are charged some percentage of their total contributed money (paid premiums) at termination. The reason is because it is a breach of contract when this happens.

Maturity

Maturity as a term use in insurance is the time a policy is due for claim. It is the time that a customer can claim his benefits. If a policyholder buy endowment/investment product with an insurance company which is expected to be due for claim in five years, that five years becomes the maturity time. Example, in FBN Insurance, if a policyholder buys a Flexible Education plan which the minimum maturity time is 5 years on March 4, 2019, the maturity of the policy will be March 3, 2024. This is when the policyholder chooses to save for just five years for the education of the child.

Due diligence form: In many insurance companies, no insurance proposal form is submitted without being accompanied by due diligence form. Due diligence form is a form that summarizes any insurance plan to the prospect which includes the maturity year of the contract, minimum premium to be paid, and the charges involved at termination in any particular year before maturity. Once a prospect signs the form and becomes a policyholder, everything stated on the form is binding on him. He consents that he agrees with the terms and conditions of the policy once he appends his signature on the form. The form is also known as consent form. Primarily, the risk and insurance aspects of due diligence begin with an understanding of the structure of the proposed transaction (Much Shelist 2011).

Financial Advisor (FA)

The term financial advisor is an insurance agent who uses financial knowledge to sell insurance policies to people to meet a particular financial goals and he or she is assigned to a unit manager. Financial advisors are the powerhouse of every insurance company. They are the people that go out to get the prospects which after proper marketing of the products to them turn into policyholders. Insurance companies cannot function without the effective function of the financial advisors. They are sometimes commonly referred to as insurance agents. A good financial advisor gets to know you as a person along with your future goals. The advisor explores your family situation by asking questions like, "Are you married?" and "Do you have children?" (Barbara Friedberg 2018).

Cooling off period

This is the grace period in which a new policyholder with an insurance company is given the opportunity to cancel the policy he entered into and have his paid premium refunded to him. You may want to cancel an insurance policy if you have just bought it and have changed your mind. By law, you have a minimum 14-day cooling-off period during which you can cancel the policy for any reason. If you've bought life insurance, the cooling-off period is 30 days. Many people cool off their policy when they start having doubts after signing in to any insurance policy and therefore decide to cancel it. This happens when the policy is not fully in force.

Waiting period

A waiting period refers to the time an insured must wait before some or all of their coverage comes into effect. Only when the waiting period has passed can the insured have a right to file a claim for the benefits of the insurance policy.

Depending on any insurance company and the regulatory body of insurance in any country, some have their waiting period as three months. In this period, the company will not pay any death claim or death benefit to the beneficiary if the policyholder dies.

According to Dan Cody of Pivot Insurance, United States, a waiting period means that there is a specific period of time, such as one or two years, where the insurance company will only pay the dollar amount of premiums that have been paid into the policy to the beneficiaries. As an example let's say a person has a $100,000 term life insurance policy that has a two year waiting period.

If the insured person passes away during those 2 years the beneficiary will only receive the total of the premiums that have been paid up to this point. In this scenario, the beneficiaries will not receive the full $100,000 payout (Dan Cody 2014).

Endowment plan

This is an insurance plan that allows the policyholder to save for future. Many commercial banks are into this kind of insurance but the banks operate the insurance as a subsidiary to the bank holdings. In this type of insurance, the insured do not need to die before claim is made unlike in pure life insurance packages. Endowment plans are also called investment plans. An endowment plan, on the other hand, is a combination of investment and insurance. In other words, an endowment plan allows you to save for future (Santosh Agarwal 2017). We will be making use of this term in the subsequent chapters of this book.

Term Plan

Term plan is a pure risk product of insurance companies. It is one of the oldest types of insurance policies. It is the kind of life insurance that the policyholder must die before claim is paid. This is the type of insurance plan that many people know about. Term plan offers no long-term savings options. If you buy a term plan, the beneficiaries will receive the guaranteed death benefit only in case of your untimely demise.

References

- 123 Money Ltd (2014), What is a proposal form?, published by 123 Money Ltd, Dundrum, Dublin, Ireland
- Baker, M (1992), Marketing Strategy and Management, Published by Palgrave, New York, United States
- Barbara, F (2018), What Do Financial Advisors Do? Everything You Need to Know, published by Smart Asset, New York City, United States
- Isaac, N (2014), The role of the proposal form in an insurance agreement, published by Daily Nation, Nairobi, Kenya
- Julia, K (2019), Insurance Premium, published by Investopedia, New York, United States
- Kingstons, C (2011), Marine Insurance in Philadelphia During the Quasi-War with France, 1795–1801, published by Cambridge University Press, United Kingdom
- MedIndia (2016), Sum Assured and Maturity Value, published by MedIndia, Anna Nagar, India
- Much Shelist (2011), Insurance and Due Diligence in the Business Transaction, published by Much Law, Chicago, United States
- Mundy C (2011), Enterprise risk: who knows my business better than me, Published by MCB UP Ltd, United Kingdom
- Prem J (2018), What is the difference between, an insurer and insured?, published by Quora, California, United States

- Santosh Agarwal (2017), Endowment Plans Vs Term Plans - Which insurance plan is better?, published by Living Media India Limited, India
- Trusted Choice Life Insurance (2013), Best Way To Choose a Life Insurance Beneficiary, published by Trusted Choice Life Insurance, Cambodia
- Uzochukwu Mike P (2019), Choosing and Working as an Insurance Agent, published by Smart Connect, Delta State, Nigeria

Chapter 3

Sum Assured

Sum assured is an important term used in insurance. Different policyholders have different sum assured. A policyholder can have a high sum assured or a lesser one depending on his or her financial strength and other factors.

The sum assured is the amount of money an insurance policy guarantees to pay up before any bonuses are added. In other words, sum assured is the guaranteed amount the policyholder will receive. This is also known as the cover or the coverage amount and is the total amount for which an individual is insured. Under every life insurance documentation a particular sum assured is declared by the insured which is paid at the Maturity or in the event of death of the insured to the beneficiary. Sum Assured can also be called a life cover or Death Benefit protection (Easy Policy 2012).

The sum assured is the amount of money an insurance policy guarantees to pay up before any bonuses are added. In other words, sum assured is the guaranteed amount the policyholder will receive (MedIndia 2016). According to Prakarsh Gagdani, sum assured in insurance company assures to pay a person in case of any claim (Prakarsh Gagdani 2016). From the view of Aastha Insurance Brokers Pvt. Ltd, sum assured = value of insurance cover provided to you at time of buying the contract (Aastha Insurance Brokers Pvt. Ltd 2017).

According to FBN Insurance, the formula for calculation of the sum assured of life insurance businesses is given as:

Sum Assured = premium/rate x 1000.

Premium = The amount of money the policyholder agrees to be paying to keep the policy force. Premium can be paid once, annually, half yearly, quarterly or monthly.

Rate = factor that determines whether the sum assured will be high or low. Rates are stated on rate table and sometimes controlled by the body that regulates insurance companies operation in any country. A rate is a number.

1000 = a constant factor.

3.1 Factors Affecting Sum Assured

There are a number of factors that affects the sum assured of a policyholder. If you are making plan to buy any insurance policy, more importantly endowment or any life insurance policy, make sure you take these factors into consideration.

Doing this will guide you on the right time to buy any policy under any insurance company. That your sum assured stated $2,000,000 at the initial calculation does not guarantee the same amount at maturity or claim if you do not maintain some standards.

Age of the Policyholder

Age is an important factor in choosing any insurance life policy and it still affects the sum assured of the holder. In your 20s, life insurance is inexpensive and easy to get. At this age, you can expect an enormous number of term life options at affordable prices (Jeff Rose 2019).

As the age of the insured increases, the sum assured decreases. If there are two policyholders that pay the same premium monthly and they picked the policy the same day (for life insurance), and of different ages, the younger will have higher sum assured than the older. The reason is because as someone becomes old, he or she is closer to the grave. Because of this, the insurance company bears higher risk than when the person is younger.

So, if you have someone holding same endowment policy with you in the same office and paying the same premium but you found out that the person was paid higher than you at maturity, just know that one of the factors that may cause that is difference in age.

If Mr Anthony picks an endowment policy which is under life insurance for monthly premium of $25 and he is of age 21 years for 10 years. And Mr Roberts who is of age 40 years picks the same endowment plan for $25 monthly premium for 10 years as well and the same day.

Mr Anthony's sum assured will be higher than that of Mr Roberts because he is younger. That means that at maturity time of 10 years, Mr Anthony will be paid higher than Roberts.

Premium

What is your premium like? Is your premium higher than that of another person that is into the same insurance contract with you? When you pay higher premium than another person, you will have higher sum assured. The choice of premium amount is what insurance prospects should look into before going into any plan.

It is advisable for insurance consumers to pay higher premiums if they have the capacity at the commencement of any insurance plan. Many prospects are always asking the question "what is the minimum premium?" Do not settle for the less in any way. Though some agents will be happy for you to pay high premium but it is good if you can do that. Do not opt in for lowest premium of $14 monthly if you can pay $25 monthly.

If you pay high, your sum assured will be high. Also, it will make you to be able to invest reasonable amount of money in the case of choosing insurance plans. A policyholder that pays higher premiums will also have higher interest and bonuses.

Duration

How long you choose to take any life insurance product matters a lot. If a customer chooses to run a particular policy for minimum duration of 6 year and another customer decides to pick the same plan for 15 year at the same premium and same age, the return at maturity or claim will not be same. In the other words, the longer the duration, the higher the sum assured.

Sometimes, agents meet prospects and advice them to save for longer terms in one or two endowment plans. They do this not because they just want to earn higher commissions because of the long duration but also to make the customer have higher sum assured at maturity. Also, the insurance company add more bonuses to customers that invest for longer time than those that opt in for short number of year or years.

Insurance companies on their own are made up of businessmen and women. In respect to that, when a customer agrees to pick an investment plan for long time at the commencement of the policy, they are happy that they will do more business with the premium paid by the plan holder. They invest the premiums into good businesses that give them more profits.

Because of the more profit they will make from the longer term endowment of policyholders, they give such customers higher sum assured. If you are a capable individual planning to pick any endowment plan from any insurance company of your choice, it will be good you go higher than the minimum duration stated by such plan. If such plan states that the minimum maturity duration of the endowment plan is 5 years, you can pick the plan for 10 years. It is quite okay.

Civil servants that are planning to pick a plan to save towards retirement should not be so quick to opt in for the minimum duration. If they have higher duration in service, they should go for longer duration. That will make them save more money and at the same time have more bonuses added at maturity. It is better to be patient and have more money in return than to enter into insurance contract for short time and have yourself paid just peanut at maturity. Save longer and have something tangible at the end.

Mode of Payment

Insurance policies give room for payment mode. The mode can be monthly, quarterly, half yearly, yearly or single premium. The payment mode chosen by the policyholder has a way of affecting the sum assured after its calculation.

If a customer has its payment mode as single, the sum assured cannot be same when another customer of the same age decides to have his own payment to be monthly. The gap between the two assured sums is very high in some cases. The reason is that if a good business individual is given huge amount of money to start selling products, his profit cannot be the same with someone that is given about 0.02 of the same amount every month to run the same kind of business.

Single premium payment is when a customer decides to pay huge amount of money once to get an insurance cover. It can also be called lump-sum payment. Some customers who are financially buoyant enough make once payment for insurance purchase. The sum assured obtained in single premium payment is higher.

If a policyholder for instance starts an investment policy with $1,000,000 with Aastha Insurance Brokers Pvt. Ltd as a single premium for five years, the sum assured that the holder will claim at maturity will not be same with that of a customer that chooses to be making monthly payment of $16,666.67 for the same five years plan. In single premium, the policyholder pays a huge premium once and keeps the money with insurance till maturity. But in monthly payment, the insured makes an instalment payment every month. When lump sum or single premium is paid, the insurance company has more money in their pool of wealth. So, sum assured of single premium is higher than when payment is made by instalment to meet the same amount of money given as single at the maturity of the policy.

Consistency in Premium Payment

If you are policyholder or a prospect planning to pick any insurance plan, it is important that how consistent you pay your premium is fundamental. If at the start of the policy that you agree to be making your payment every month, ensure to maintain such agreed standard. If you default after some time, your sum assured calculated at the initiation of the policy can be affected.

Any insured that does not meet up with constant payment of the premium agreed at the beginning of the policy should know that his or her sum assured can be reduced at the maturity of the policy. Maybe at the beginning, you agreed to be paying $20 every month but fail along the line, your sum assured cannot be the same again. The reason is that you are no longer keeping to the agreement which was reached between you and the insured at the start.

Also, you can get charged from the other premiums you will pay because you defaulted. That charge may not show in your policy statement when the policy is still in force but at the maturity or during claim. When the claim is processed, you will discover that the money reduce from the initial calculated sum assured. So, consistency in premium payment is needed for you to have your exact sum assured maintained.

Agents may not tell you about this so that you do not have doubt in signing insurance contract. But in the world of insurance, the truth remains that your sum assured can be reduced if you do not pay your premiums as of when due. But, you do not need to be afraid because the charge will not be much when you default.

3.2 Recalculation of Sum Assured

In the world of insurance and risk management sum assured can be recalculated. This recalculation of sum assured occurs under some conditions. No policyholder of an insurance company will be happy to be short paid and because of this recalculation is important in some cases. But it is not sum assured of all policies that maintained some criteria are recalculated. There are conditions for that and we are covering those conditions in this section.

Conditions for recalculation of Sum Assured

The two major reasons or conditions for recalculation of sum assured are as follows:

(1) Increase in Premium payment

(2) Decrease in premium

(3) When the total Contribution is higher than the initial sum assured

Increase in Premium payment

Insurance is an organized profession and wants everything to be as planned. Because of the orderliness in insurance, insurance industry does not want to speak much grammar with their product consumers. To this effect, there is room for recalculation of sum assured in the case of increase in the premium agreed to be paying at commencement.

If an insured picks a life insurance plan and signed that he would be paying a particular amount of money every month but in the course of the payment starts paying more than he supposed to, there will be recalculation of sum assured. The same thing still applies in general insurance businesses. But the company and the policyholder do not want to lose.

Sometimes, the administrators at the individual offices of the insurance company are assigned to call you to know why you pay more than the agree premium at the agreed mode of payment, maybe monthly, quarterly, half yearly and yearly. After hearing from you that you do that maybe because you earn more than you were earning from your place of work, they instruct you to write a letter for increase in premium and scan to them or submit to any of their branches close to you. With the letter written and signed by you, you have given the company the go ahead order to increase your premium.

As the premium is increased, your sum assured is recalculated to meet the increase. When you do this, it will maintain smooth running of the plan you have with the company. When the sum is calculated, the insured is sometimes notified of the changes. This can be through SMS or email notification.

Some agents contribute to the recalculation of sum assured due to increase in premium payment. The reason is because since the job is a commission based, they advise the customers that they can pay more than the premium they agreed to be paying at the beginning of the policy. They do this so that when the policyholders pay more, they make more money for themselves. Though a policyholder paying more premium than one agreed at the start of the policy is not bad because they at the same time can save more money than what they planned before for endowment policies. Also, when the technical administrators call from regional or head offices in respect to the increase of the premium, the agents helps in writing the letter that the insured will sign for the increase in premium to match the new sum assured that will be recalculated by the technical.

Decrease in premium

In life, sometimes things change from good to bad. Also, people sometimes have more demand from people than the ones they were getting before. There are people whose financial responsibilities have increased over the years unlike what they were having before. Increase in financial responsibility can make someone to have less to use or invest into insurance plan.

Because of the higher responsibility and demand by other needs, many call their financial advisors to reduce their premium payment. Maybe the policyholder was paying $100 monthly, he may end up reducing the premium of the policy to $30 every month. Doing this can enable him meet up with the premium payment without much stress. It saves him the weakness of allowing the policy to lapse due to not making any payment at all for his policy.

So, if you are a prospect considering of picking any insurance plan with good amount of money, feel free to do that. Do not be worried so much on whether you can meet up with the premium you choose because there can be room for reduction so far not below the minimum premium stated by the company. Even if you marry tomorrow and there is financial burden on you, you can still reduce your premium. Your sum assured can be recalculated as well to suit the reduction you will make.

Bad economy at the same time can be a contributor to reduction in premium of many policyholders. Maybe the insured was doing well in his business and made more gains, if the economy becomes bad, he can call for reduction of his premium. Many people from different parts of the world have been hit hard by bad economy and it made many reduce their premiums with insurance companies while some persons quit totally. Some salary earning workers have had their salaries reduced in countries that are experiencing economic meltdown.

No matter what the factors may be, there is always recalculation of sum assured anytime there is reduction in monthly, quarterly, half yearly or yearly premium. This maintains orderliness and makes the policy to continue to be in force. When the recalculation is carried out, the new sum assured becomes lesser than the former when the premium was high.

When the Total Contribution is higher than the Initial Sum Assured

For every premium paid by the insured, they are monitored by the administrators. They watch these payments until they mature. As the money is paid into the account of the insurance company, they do their work with time to allocate the money to the policy. This with time shows in the statement of the policyholder.

Insurance companies do not reject money paid into their account by the holder of any insurance plan with their company unless in rare occasion maybe due to overage. In fact, these companies need more money to do more businesses. They need more to be in their money pool. It will push them to be more financially buoyant and be able to run the company without fear.

Let's say that a policyholder registers for an endowment product and agreed to be paying $5,000 monthly with FBN Insurance for five years. With this agreement, the sum assured was calculated at it gave the result of $310, 777.66. That means the sum assured the policyholder will get at maturity will be $310, 777.66. Maybe along the line the life of the policyholder improves financially and he them contributes $500,000 in three years which is higher than the initial sum assured calculated and this happens even before maturity.

He contributes this amount of money in just three years and even has two years left before the policy matures. In the other words, he is likely to even have more than times two of the initial sum assured at maturity. Because of this new development and outburst in the contribution which is even much higher than the sum assured, his sum assured is recalculated and then given a new value at maturity.

3.3 The use of Sum Assured in Policies

In insurance, the term "sum assured" can be used in such a way that an ordinary person that is not in insurance sector may not understand. The use of the term can be confusing in such a way that the insurance buyer may think that the sum assured as stated in the policy pack implies the interest he or she will get at the maturity of his or her endowment policy.

Some agents do not help in making their customers understand that the term is sometimes used just in respect to the product design. Some of these agents are just after making sales. Whether the buyer understands the use of the term in the key statements in the form is none of their businesses. They end up deceiving these innocent men and women just because they want to make sales.

The customer becomes disappointed at the policy maturity when they find out that the agent lied to him. It makes many get discouraged when it comes to buying another insurance product. We will give instance in this section concerning what we are talking about.

Example of the use of Sum Assured

Here, example where sum assured is used as if it's interest in an endowment plan will be narrated. In summary, that is not interest but means through which the contribution made by the policyholder will be paid as the plan approaches maturity. This example is sourced from Cash Flow endowment plan of First Bank of Nigeria Insurance (FBN Insurance). Only a truthful financial advisor can tell you what this implies in detail. The narration goes thus:

FBNInsurance FlexiCash is an endowment plan that allows the policyholder live life to the fullest today and at the same time stay protected by allowing for the flexibility of receiving a specified percentage of the sum assured at specified intervals.

Maturity Benefits:

Policyholder gets periodic cashflow as described below:

- 25% of the sum assured will be paid at the end of the fourth year
- 25% of the sum assured will be paid mid-way through the outstanding duration after the first payment
- 100% of the sum assured plus all accrued bonuses will be paid at maturity.

From the above narration on the benefits of the FlexiCash plan, someone who do not have good experience in insurance may think that it means 25% interest will be added to his total contribution at the end of the fourth year. No. It is not so. It means that 25% of the calculated sum assured at the beginning of the policy will be paid to the policyholder at the end of the fourth year. In this flexiCash plan, the sum assured is usually less than the total contribution the holder is to make at the end of the maturity year. That is six years or more than depending on the choice of the customer. FlexiCash endowment plan of FBN Insurance has a minimum maturity time of six years.

The same 25% of the sum assured of the policy is paid to the policyholder at the end of the fifth year if the plan is to be taken for six years. At the end of the sixth year, hundred percent of the sum assured is paid to the policyholder. This makes the total payment the customer receives plus some other bonuses.

References

- Aastha Insurance Brokers Pvt. Ltd (2017), What does sum assured means?, published by Aastha Insurance Brokers Pvt. Ltd, India
- Easy Policy (2012), How to Calculate the Sum Assured Required in Life Insurance?, published by Easy policy, Noida, Uttar Pradesh, India
- MedIndia (2016), Sum Assured and Maturity Value, published by MedIndia, Anna Nagar, India
- Much Shelist (2011), Insurance and Due Diligence in the Business Transaction, published by Much Law, Chicago, United States
- Prakarsh Gagdani (2016), What does sum assured means?, published by Quora, California, United States
- FBN Insurance (2019), Calculation of Sum Assured, published by FBN Insurance, Marina, Lagos State, Nigeria
- FBN Insurance (2019), FlexiCash, published by First Bank of Nigeria Insurance, Marina, Lagos State.
- Jeff Rose (2019), Life Insurance Rates By Age, published by Good Financial Cents, California, United States

Chapter 4

Insincerity among Insurance Agents

They may tell you lies because they want to make sales. Some after the whole lie end up not being able to close the business because there are prospects that easily differentiate truth from lie. Many agents usually say they cannot make sales without lying to their prospects.

Some agents have taken lying as nothing. Some see it as normal thing every man has to live with. They can tell you that you earn the whole interest in the world by opting in to any plan they market. All are just fake comments. If you are a prospect trying to pick any savings plan with any insurance company, do not put interest first. That should not be your priority. This is an advice from someone that has been in the job for years.

4.1 Why do some Insurance Agents lie a lot?

There are reasons why some of these gentlemen and women do this. It is not as if all the agents in insurance business do this but some. There are many that are still clean.

These are clean financial advisors that prefer to protect their integrity than make sales anyhow. We will be discussing why many insurance agents are not sincere in this section. Why insincerity among some agents in insurance are as follow:

(1) They are on target

(2) The quest to earn huge commission

(3) Competition with other agents

They are on target

Have you worked with any company before where it is all about meeting the company's target? Your manager is always all over you like fly hitting you with harsh words because he wants you to meet your target. Even when you are home to rest, he also calls you telling you to make sure you meet your target or otherwise you are 'flushed' out of the company.

Insurance job is a target based job. Because of this, many agents chose to lie to their prospects to close businesses instead of getting lashing words from their unit managers. To such agents, they may be thrown off balance if they lose their job because they do not meet target. It is the job and a lot have adopted the attitude of being insincere during sales.

Some managers that are in charge of financial advisors do not know how to carry out their official activities properly. They can insult you, your wife and even your entire family because you are not productive in the insurance business you do.

Some agents do not sleep at home properly because of the insults they receive from their manager as they do not meet their target. When they are on their beds to sleep those insulting words keep on playing in their memories continuously. It is one of the bad sides of working as an insurance agent.

If you do not hold yourself as an agent and allow the harsh words of your manager disturb you much, you end up miss-selling insurance services. The bad thing is that these managers sometimes deny their agents when complain of mis-selling gets to the head office desk filed by the customers. The customers that insurance agents sold insurance products in a wrong way sometimes call head office of the insurance company to complain of how they were deceived by salespersons of the company.

This is not far from the statement of Akosha desk office as she stated "I may not have gone so far. Every week, hundreds of mis-selling and dishonest insurance agents-related complaints land on our desks at Akosha. The sheer number and magnitude of these complaints in itself is a proof of the extent to which this racket is flourishing in the country" (Akosha 2012).

The quest to earn Huge Commission

Commission is fee paid to an agent or insurance salesperson as a percentage of the policy premium. The percentage varies widely depending on coverage, the insurer, and the marketing methods (Money Control 2019). Premium paid on life insurance policies are usually higher than that of general policies in some cases. Commission keeps agents going as it puts food on the table of salespersons.

The joy of every agent working in insurance company is to see his commission grow. If the commission is not going high or growing gradually, he is not always happy. Some agents have accused the insurance companies for sidelining some part of their commission because they believe they do not receive what they suppose to get when paid. Attitude of this type has made many agents feel like quitting the jobs they do as salesperson.

But on a serious note, there are some insurance companies that are not transparent in their payment of commission. Some do not pay the agents the amount of commission they suppose to earn from the premiums paid by their customers. This brings the morale of some of the workers. Transparency is an important factor in insurance companies.

Even as many agents in insurance are not favoured by good commission, some are still striving to make things work out better. This has pushed a lot of them to sell insincerely to meet up and have better commission. They do this with combination of different kinds of lies just to make their money grow in the industry. Some who earn less than others are not happy with themselves. They want increase. They want to make more money for themselves.

Those in banking which is also under the umbrella of finance earn well and they are on fixed salary. On the other hand, there are banks that run insurance company as a subsidiary of one of the company's holding. Sometimes, the agents compare their commission with the salaries of these bankers. A banker in United States of America earns between $25,991 - $52,865 monthly.

When agents do not earn close or more than bankers in any society they do find themselves, they are not always happy. They feel they are wasting their time in the company. For them to cover up and meet up with the commission they desire, they end up mis-selling to meet up with the standard. It is only those that are disciplined and understand that insincerity is not good that make effort to sell the insurance services handed to them rightly.

Have you ever filled a proposal form of an investment plan in any insurance office with the aim to save for specific years and later found out that the maturity date changed? Sometimes you discover the increase in the maturity date when you come for your statement. It does not mean that the increase in the maturity year which you filled at the commencement of the policy changed due to error. Most of the changes in the date of maturity are intentional actions engineered by insurance salespersons.

Take for example that a customer registered for a five years investment plan and stated 5 years in the duration section. The intention of this kind of customer is to make claim at the end of five years. But instead of this to remain, some agents end up altering the date. Some agents sometimes increase the number to ten years.

Why the increase in the number of years? They do this because they want to earn higher commission as the customer pays his premiums.

In some investment policies for example, the increase from five years to ten years means extra 5 percent increase in the commission rate. Normal five years duration is 10% on the premium paid by the customer. Increasing the duration to ten years mean 15% commission rate on the premium paid by the customer but it all depends on the insurance company.

A customer who pays $5,000 for monthly premium for duration of 5 years in endowment plan makes the agent earn $500 as commission on the premium for the first year. But if the agent lifts the duration to ten years, his commission is $750 for 15% rate for the first year. But this percentage is dependent on the kind of product and the company as well.

The increase is insincere games that financial advisors play. It has been robbing a lot of insurance companies till date. Many agents want to earn more money in the company and hence keep filling some information different from what the customers filled at commencement. It is a dirty game played by many agents. All policyholders should always do well to monitor their policies to make sure that the duration they filled is still the same.

Competition with other Agents

In any insurance unit managed by one manager, there are always top sellers. These are people whose performances are exceptional. They are the pillars of the unit. Before five best salespersons in the unit are called, their names must be called.

They are called the powerhouse of the unit they belong to. They are the champions of the group they represent. Their managers usually advice the less performing financial advisors to be like such salespersons. Their productions every week are usually the highest.

Because these agents do exceptionally well, with time jealousy begin to grow among them. Every one of them always wants to be on the top. Each wants to be the number one in the group.

The jealousy now gives birth to competition among them. Everyone keeps making effort to make greater sales within the shortest time. As a result of this, many say both what the company told them to say and what they were not instructed to. Sometimes they give higher interest rate or sum assured to their prospects because they want to be on the top. Competition becomes top thing among the salespersons.

References

- Akosha (2012), 5 Shocking mis-selling tricks used by insurance agents, published by Akosha, India
- Money Control (2019), Commission, published by Money Control, India

Chapter 5

Buying Insurance Policies and Signing Terms and Conditions

It is important to buy insurance for risk management. It is also good to be safe as you are covered against the unplanned and unforeseen circumstances that may happen in life. But in doing all these things, do them carefully. Virtually all insurance policies contain conditions, which are rules of the policy (Marianne Bonner 2018).

In the developed countries of the world, insurance sells very well. This is quite different from the sale of the similar services in Africa. One of the reasons is because the Continent does not know much about insurance policies. Also, some are afraid because of the bad experience their loved ones had in the past when it comes to paying of claims. But no matter how it is, insurance services in Africa are improving over the years and people now buy more insurance than in the past.

Every insurance policy has terms and conditions or due diligence. Sometimes agents convince the customers to sign these terms and conditions without going through that section properly. Sometimes there is delicate information hidden in the section. But most insurance prospects are not aware of this.

Though the agents will explain the policy to you to your understanding, it is also important you check the terms and conditions before signing. It should not be all about sign here, sign here and you rush and sign the form. Even if the agent explains everything to you, there is still need for you to read properly and ask questions at the end.

Be it general insurance or life insurance policy, do not rush and sign the contract. It may not take you more than 5 to 10 minutes to go through the due diligence form. You may discover some other things you do not know about the insurance policy when you read properly. It is better to know some new things than to rush and sign and start making baseless cases tomorrow.

5.1 Why you should Read Insurance Policies Terms and Conditions (T & C)

(1) To know if charges Apply
(2) To understand the plan
(3) For legal binding

To know if Charges Apply

It is hard to see any insurance policy that does not charge if the holder of the policy wants to terminate the policy before its maturity. Anytime any client wants to close his or her policy before its maturity time, it is called termination.

Depending on the duration (years) the customer's policy has been in force, the policyholder can be charged from his or her own total contributed premiums since the policy has been in force. But many customers do not know about this.

The charges a customer receive at the termination of any policy before maturity is called the surrender charges. But some customers do not know about these charges because they did not go through the due diligence form before signing. They feel bad when they are faced with challenges that move them to ask for the money they saved with investment plan of any insurance company.

If it is five years endowment plan, the surrender charge if the customer who have saved for more than one year but less than two years can be as high as 40% of his total contribution. But if he has read through the terms and conditions at the commencement of the policy, he would have known about this beforehand. As a prospect or policyholder, it is your duty to go through the terms and conditions binding on any policy you want to buy. It is a good way of avoiding showering of insult on your financial advisor in case of any challenge that moves you to withdraw from any policy you are running.

All insurance policies include terms and conditions that describe the ways in which the policy will operate and specify what is included and what is not, what the insurance company promises to do and what the policyholder promises to do. Terms and conditions are fundamental components of the insurance contract. If you do not comply with the terms and conditions of the policy, you may be in breach of the contract with the insurer. This may mean that the insurer is not obliged to fulfil its promise and pay out some or all of your claim (Insurance Council of Australia 2013).

From the above sentences from Insurance Council of Australia, it is clear that Terms and Conditions cover a lot. These much he covers is what the insured should know to know what the company cannot do for him if he decides to leave before maturity. Also, terms and conditions instruct the policyholder on what he or she will lose if he leaves before maturity. It is a two way thing. It is either the insured looses or gain. In respect to that, surrender charges awaits him if he or she decides to quit the contract early. In terms insurance policies, he will not get any cover if he refuses to pay his premium or goes contrary to what is stated in the terms and conditions.

Do not expect any financial advisor to start reading surrender charges to you when you come to buy any insurance packages. It will not make sense as many will not buy insurance if the surrender charges are echoed. The thing is that the agent tells you the basic things about the policy. One of them will be that you have to save for at least five years before you have access to the money and the interest for investment policies.

What shall it profit a policyholder to rush and sign insurance contract and feels bad later because of charges? If you want to be aware of charges, endeavour to read through the due diligence. It is very important but many insured have neglected it over the years.

To understand the plan

Understanding of whatever thing someone is doing is very important. If you understand what you do in life as a person, it makes you have clearer view of where you are going. Understanding it will open your eyes to newer ideas and make you much better.

If you are insuring your home, your insurer may ask how old the property is, whether it has been well maintained, and the construction materials (such as roofing) used. All these still boil down to understanding. You have to know deep things about what you are doing or planning to do. So do not allow anyone deceive you. Read it well.

Reading through terms and conditions of an insurance policy helps the prospects to see terms used in insurance. When they see these terms and do not understand them, it moves them to ask questions. Asking questions about the terms lead to explanation. And at the end, it adds to the knowledge of the policyholder.

There are many people that do not know that they will lose some of the benefits of a policy when it lapses. This information is usually found in the terms and conditions. But some customers do not know about this because they do not read before signing into any insurance plan. You broaden your knowledge when you read.

What of death benefit of an insurance plan? What is the period the beneficiaries should come for the claim? These are some sensitive areas in insurance that agents may sometimes forget to tell you when selling insurance to you. So go through the terms and conditions guiding the insurance plan you are going into to know these things.

In pure life insurance products which are considered pure risk packages, there is time limit a beneficiary or the beneficiaries are expected to contact the insurer in the event of the death of the insured. But many people including policyholders and beneficiaries are not aware of this. Some have lost claim benefits entitled to them in the event of the death of the policyholders because they do not report to the insurance company at the specified time in the policy terms and conditions.

Some life insurance policies categorically stated that the family or the beneficiaries to the life assured must report the death of the insured within one year of the occurrence. To this effect, the beneficiaries can claim the death benefits of their dead loved ones. The life insured sometimes when buying life insurance policy do not know about this to make it known to the family he belongs to before that. The cause can be the improper study of the terms and conditions guiding the policy.

In some cases, it is usually already late before the family discovers and report to the insurance company. The insurance company after critical examination finds out that the grace period has passed and therefore refuses to pay claim. This has caused a lot of problems in the insurance industry but the fault is usually from the policyholders when they were alive.

For legal binding

Legal binding is common legal phrase indicating that an agreement has been consciously made, and certain actions are now either required or prohibited. That is to say that you consent to everything in the policy. So before you sign, make sure that you read properly so that you do not go back to the insurance company tomorrow and start making a baseless case.

Sometimes some customers threaten to sue insurance companies but end up losing the case. In the course of the court judgement, the insurance company provides when the customer signed at the beginning of the policy. The judge looks into these documents and at the end the customer lost the case. As a person planning to enter into any insurance contract, endeavour to understand the terms and conditions so that you do not fool yourself in court of law when issues arise.

References

- Insurance Council of Australia (2013), Understand your Insurance Policy, published by Insurance Council of Australia, Sydney NSW, Australia
- Marianne Bonner (2018), What are Insurance Conditions? Published by The Balance Small Business, New York City, United States

Chapter 6

Insurance Policies and Interest

The agents and insurance companies can paint pictures. They can take their customers on a ride and make them see the beauty in insurance policies though insurance policies are really good. Insurance policies are good if you understand the essence in which the products were designed in the first place.

Insurance companies are not money bags. If you are looking at the company as one that has all the money and you will get whole lot of interest from them, you are really making a lot of mistakes. You will end up being disappointed.

Irrespective of how beautiful any insurance company may design their products, do not put all your hope in the "interest zone". Some products are designed with good interest rate but do not have it as the priority. Interest giving should not be the priority.

In some endowment plans, there may be interests in the name of bonuses that are given at maturity. This is in line with the words of Policy Bazaar statements.

"Endowment – with Profit: in this type of policy the nominee receives sum assured plus bonuses for the number of years the policy was in force in case of the policy holder\'s death. In case of survival up to the policy term the insured receives sum assured plus bonus for the term of the policy (Policy Bazaar 2019)"

6.1 Underpayment can be experienced

Have you ever think of underpayment while registering for any insurance endowment plan? It is important you think of underpayment as well and not just the huge financial claim you will make at maturity with interest. A wise man does not just think of gain alone but also loss. So do not be surprised if someone told you that he was underpaid by one insurance company when he or she bought investment policy from the company.

Conditions for Underpayment at Maturity of an Endowment Policy

There are conditions policyholders are underpaid at the maturity of their insurance policy. Here we will be discussing these conditions properly.

The conditions for underpayment in investment and savings plan in insurance companies are

(1) Low premium payment when compared with the risk cover of the plan

(2) Old age of the customer

(3) Inconsistency in premium payment

Low Premium Payment when compared with the Risk cover of the Plan

Most times when life insurance policies are marketed to prospects, the question they usually ask is what is the least monthly premium? The reason for that is that they want to know if it is what they can do and also to go for the least monthly premium. But little do they know that they may be underpaid at maturity when they registered for endowment plan or insurance savings plan.

In insurance savings plan that has high risk cover, the customer can be paid less than the total money he contributed at the end of the policy. Let me use "Easy Save" Savings plan of FBN Insurance as an example. The policy has a risk cover of five thousand naira (N5,000). That currency naira is that of Nigeria. The risk covers the policyholder for death. In the case of death of the policy holder, the beneficiary is entitled to five hundred naira (N500,000) on the five thousand naira paid for the risk.

If a policyholder wants to be paying just five thousand naira every month as the monthly premium, he will pay ten thousand naira (N10,000) for a start. From this analysis, five thousand naira is invested and the other five thousand naira for risk cover. Easy Save is just one year saving plan of the company. If at the end of the one year and the customer does not die, the risk cover is not going to be refunded. Let us say that at the end of the year that the contributed total of N65, 000 and when the N5,000 is removed, she is left with N60,000.

If the interest rate of the company is 3% of the total invested money outside the risk that is not refundable, 3% of N60,000 gives N1,800. When the N1,800 is added to the N60,000, the result becomes N61,800. That is not up to the total money the client paid including the risk.

So, underpayment shows itself here. The total money paid was N65,000 but the customer was paid total of N61,800. That is underpayment. Insurance buyers should not have interest as their priority when buying insurance policies.

Old Age of the Customer

As stated before, age factor is very important while picking any insurance policy. Be it term insurance or endowment, age is important. The age in which a customer picks insurance policy determines whether he will have good interest or bonuses paid to him or her or not. Agents do not submit any proposal form to the administrators for capturing without first calculating the sum assured which age of the customer plays important role in.

In insurance offices, argument usually arises between insurance officers and policyholders when they are short paid. Some of the short payments come because the customer signed the insurance contract when they were already getting to old age. Many do not understand that going into insurance at older age can make them have lesser pay at maturity which can even cut into their totally contributed premiums over the years.

Any person choosing endowment insurance policy that has high risk cover as from the age of 59 years is likely to be short paid at maturity. This is so because the person at that age is closer to death. That is to say that under normal circumstances, the life span of the person is not too long.

The company at that age of the customer bears higher risk. So, people that have regular salaries and want to save ahead toward one or two projects should start early enough. If they are waiting till their promotions which make them older in age, then they are likely to lose small portion of their totally contributed premiums at maturity.

Inconsistency in Premium Payment

It's not all about buying insurance. Another important thing is being consistent in your payment. Even if you miss some payments, do not miss three consecutive months. You are likely to lose some benefits attached to some policies when you do so.

Cover Hound made some statements on the bad sides of missing premium payment for home owners insurance "If you miss premium payments and your insurance is cancelled, your credit score will reflect it. This could make it tougher for you to get any other kind of credit, as well as another insurance policy. As you can see, there are many consequences of missing homeowners insurance payments—none of which are positive" (Cover Hound 2017).

Inconsistency in payment can result to shortage in payment of claim to policyholders or beneficiaries at maturity or death of the holder. In endowment life insurance plans, customers are charged from their premiums if they fail to pay premiums consistently or when due.

This may not show when the policy is still in force but when matured and due for claim. If you are a policyholder in any insurance company, always pay your premiums to avoid discrepancy at maturity.

6.2 Choosing to Pay Higher Premium

How much premium are you planning to be paying to insurance company on monthly or yearly basis? Is the premium high or low? Do you think that such premium you choose suits you or you just want to be paying the way others do?

If you have the capacity, do not go for the lowest of the premium. Always avoid going for the lowest premium because you may end up having something lower than you expected to have at the maturity of your policy. Going for the low premium payment will give you or your beneficiaries low return.

If you want to sign up for term insurance to cover your family at the point of your death, why go for low premium when you know you have large family? Not that you just have large family but you know you can do something higher comfortably. Do not limit yourself to the lowest. The higher premium you pay, the higher coverage your family receives in the event of death.

Prospects who started with lower monthly payment can call their financial advisors or agents for increase in their monthly premium. Increase is a way to have higher bonuses added to your policy at maturity by the insurance company. Instead of disturbing any insurance company for short payment at maturity, increase your premium to have higher return if you have the resources to do so.

Insurers use premiums to cover liabilities associated with the policies they underwrite. They may also invest the premium to generate higher returns and offset some of the costs of providing the insurance coverage, which can help an insurer keep prices competitive. So, when you pay higher premium in term, investment, and general insurance policies, you have higher bonuses when you are paid at maturity or in the event of the damages covered. The higher you give, the higher you receive. There is how high a customer's premiums will be, he may not feel the charge that may occur in his policy when he is inconsistent in payment for endowment plans.

References

- Cover Hound (2017), The Consequences of Missing Homeowners Insurance Premium Payments, published by Cover Hound Inc., San Francisco, California, United States
- Policy Bazaar (2012), Endowment Policy, published by Policy Bazaar, Gurgaon, Haryana, India

Chapter 7

Insurance Product Design

Sometimes it is good to buy different insurance products from different companies. The reason is to compare to know the one that is better than the other. Also, there are some things that you may like in one product of a company that may not be in that of another company.

Also, some insurance services may look similar in name but the level of risk coverage varies per company. Every good insurance company have some unique features in their products that are not in other companies that have similar product. That at that point becomes their selling point.

Insurance products are insurance products anywhere in the world but some have something different within them. Company A may design their products in a way the client will get charged if he wants to opt out of the policy in anytime less than four years that the policy has been in force.

But company B can design the same product in such a way that the policyholder will not get charged even if he wants to opt out from the second year since the policy has been in force. That is similar products with different design. There is competition in the market and many companies are being innovative to design their own products in a unique and more accessible way.

Underwriters do great jobs when it comes to the product of any insurance company. They properly analyze the perils their individual policies will cover and those it will not. They are always careful during the design for the company not to be at loss tomorrow. The underwriters may decline the risk or may provide a quotation in which the premiums have been loaded (including the amount needed to generate a profit, in addition to covering expenses) (Black's Law Dictionary 2012).

7.1 Examples of Different Product Designs

Here we are going to look at some designed products that are made to cover a particular area of interest to the policyholders.

Educational Insurance Policy

Education is basic and something very unique. When one is educated, he gets exposed and can communicate with people effectively. As a reader of this book, if you have not passed through certain level of schooling, you may not understand what is written in this book. Education is like a mirror through which nations see their images (Uzochukwu Mike 2014).

Because many insurance companies in the recent years discovered the need to insure future education of children, they design education policy to guarantee it. In fact, in many life insurance companies, this has been one of the most selling products in the recent years. This product gives the policyholder life cover and also make it possible for the holder to be able to save enough money towards the future education of the children and in most cases the university education of the children.

If the education of your child/ward means anything to you, then you would go the extra mile to ensure they enjoy the very best, come what may. This is what our FlexiEdu plans are all about.

FlexiEdu helps every parent/guardian plan a bright future for their child/ward no matter the uncertainties of life. This plan is open to parents/sponsors of wards/children across all levels of education - FBN Insurance.

Our Children's Education Savings Plan is an affordable means of protection, to establish a reserved pool, sufficient to make payment of school fees for your child - Zenith Prudent Insurance Company

Child education plan gives you various benefits such as life cover, building a corpus for the child's future needs and the option of adding specific riders. Go ahead and invest in an education plan, but always compare quotes before you finally sign on the dotted line - Policybazaar Insurance.

Education opens the door to brighter opportunities, but the rising cost makes it challenging for families to afford it without proper planning - Sun Life Assurance Company of Canada.

7.2 Comparing Design Benefits

Let us look at the benefit of children education insurance plan offered by FBN, Prudential Zenith, and Custodian Life Insurance. From these comparisons, you will discover the uniqueness in the design of the educational policies per the individual insurance companies.

Benefits of FlexiEdu of FBN Insurance

Maturity Benefits:

Maturity benefit is paid as a lump sum or in four (4) equal, annual installments

Death Benefits:

- In the event of the death of the policyholder before maturity, 10% of the sum assured will be payable annually to the beneficiary subject to a limit of 100% of the sum assured.
- The guaranteed maturity benefits will still be paid at maturity of the policy.
- All future premiums due for payment will be waived.

Prudential Zenith Life Insurance Children's Education Savings Plan Benefits

- Assist to save for the future quality education of the child.
- Ensures continuity of good education for the child in the event of death of the sponsor.
- It could serve as additional security to secure loan.
- The account balance is paid as sum assured or expected maximum total contribution whichever is higher.
- It is a source of emergency fund.

Custodian Life Insurance Education Endowment Benefits
- The future education of the child is secured to the tune of the targeted amount
- It qualifies for tax advantage
- At maturity, the targeted amount is payable
- Bonus declaration enhances the benefit
- Policy loan facility exists
- Collateral security
- Systematic saving vehicle

Design Comparison on the Three Polices

Name

The names of the education policies offered by the companies are individually unique. FBN Insurance calls he own FlexiEdu, Prudential Zenith name hers Children's Education Savings Plan, and Custodian Life Insurance titled theirs as Education Endowment. When agents use any of these names, you can easily detect the insurance companies they are coming from.

Other Comparisons

In FlexiEdu of FBN Insurance and in Education Endowment of Custodian Life Insurance, the premiums saved cannot be sourced from during emergency but premiums saved in Prudential Zenith Life Insurance can serve as a source of fund during emergency.

What it means is that if you opt in to save using education insurance plan, you can source money from the premiums you have saved so far if an unexpected happen under Prudential Zenith Life Insurance but for FBN Insurance and Custodian Life Insurance, you must wait until maturity or the death of the policyholder or otherwise you get charged if you want to take the money before the claim time.

In FlexiEdu of FBN Insurance, in the case of the death of the policyholder, 10% of the sum assured is paid annually to the child that stands as the beneficiary to maximum limit of 100%. For Prudential Zenith, the amount or the percentage to be paid is not specified and such option is not available in Custodian Life Insurance Education Endowment. That shows difference in design of policies by different insurance companies. That Insurance Company "A" offers the benefit you like does not imply that Company "B" will still offer same benefit. The design may resemble but not always the same.

Furthermore, Policy loan facility exists in Prudential Zenith and Custodian Life Insurance companies but such offer is not available in FBN Insurance FlexiEdu. So, if you need Policy with such feature, you consider insurance companies that have it. These clarifications show the uniqueness and variations in insurance services/products design.

7.3 Buying Insurance from Different Companies due to Design

No agent will be happy to see his customer leave the insurance company he works with to buy insurance policy from another company. The reason is simple. The agents work for their pockets. They want to make more money and grow in the company. When an agent receives less commission payment from the company he works for in a particular month, he does not feel good. Little commission payment can make an agent down for two weeks or more. The more the agent gets the more he wants. That is to show that human wants are insatiable.

Because these men are hungry in the business, they will not be happy to see you go buy insurance from another company. When you contact an agent you bought your first insurance from and inform him you would like to buy from another company, he will do anything possible to discourage you from doing that. That is one secret many policyholders or insurance prospects do not know. Even when you as a buyer tells him that there is something you like in the design of the policy of the other company, he may lie to you that his company has the feature all because he does not want you to buy from another company. He can even go further and tell you that why such benefit is not written on the policy benefits section is because there is no space on the paper.

As mentioned before, insurance products are designed with unique features. The feature company A has company B may not have. So if you see the feature you like in the product of another company. Feel free to purchase. Sometimes you may not tell your agent from the other company. But it depends on the kind of person the agent is.

The money is your money, so feel free to buy something useful with it. There is nothing wrong with having different policies with different companies. You can have five policies with three different companies. Maybe you buy 2 policies with company A, 2 with company B, and 1 with company C. At maturity of the policies, you analyse which is better. It is a good thing.

References

- Black's Law Dictionary (2012), What is Premium Loading? Definition of Premium Loading, published by Black's Law Dictionary
- FBN Insurance (2019), FlexiEdu Plan, Published by First Bank of Nigeria Insurance, Lagos State, Nigeria
- Okwuagbala Uzochukwu Mike (2014), Importance of Education to Nations, published by Hubpages Inc., California, United States
- Prudential Zenith Life Insurance (2019), Children's Education Savings Plan, published by Prudential Zenith Life Insurance, Victoria Island, Lagos, Nigeria
- Policy Bazaar (2019), Child Plans, published by Policy Bazaar Insurance Company, Gurgaon, Haryana, India
- Sun Life Assurance (2019), Education, published by Sun Life Assurance Company of Canada, Taguig City, Philippines

Chapter 8

Agents Attitude towards Policy Termination

Many people choose endowment products in insurance companies of their choice with the mindset of saving good amount of money towards the maturity of their policies. But along the line things did not work as planned. Some opted in for monthly premium payment but could not continue. Some because of much financial pressure decides to make attempt to stop. They have in their minds to continue but they could not because their financial strength was weak.

Even upon the challenges those policyholders were having, their agents kept motivating them to keep on paying their premiums no matter how the conditions were. Agents hate to see their customers coming to their offices for termination. That is their attitudes toward such move that some customers usually make. They do not want you to go irrespective of the financial challenge you face in your life.

Good salespersons are motivational teachers and speakers. Even at that moment you want to opt out from the plan you have been running, they try to motivate you. They give you reasons why you should not terminate your policy. They understand the pain you may be passing through but they do not want you to go. They do not want you to close your eyes and stop doing business with their company.

Termination means the agent stops earning from you. It means his commission starts to decrease instead of increasing. Termination has adverse effects on the agent that sold that policy to you.

So do not be surprised when an agent frown his face on hearing that you want to terminate your policy. He is trying to protect something and that is one of the reasons his attitude appears like that on hearing of termination.

8.1 Policy Termination and Agent Demotion

A demotion is a compulsory reduction in an employee's rank or job title within the organizational hierarchy of a company, public service department, or other body, unless there is no reduction in pay. Some insurance companies can demote their agents when they notice that there are many terminations in the agent's line of customers. When an agent has about 500 clients and about 300 out of such number terminates their policies within two years. That does not tell well of the agent. It sends wrong signal to the company. This sometimes makes the company invite the agent to their head office for interrogation. After meeting with the team, the agent is demoted if he or she is guilty of mis-selling. It is believed that not selling right can be the cause of many customers termination of their policies.

When insurance agents are demoted, their earnings are affected as well. Because of the fear of demotion, no agent will smile with you when you tell him you want to terminate your plan with the company. Everyone likes to move forward and not backward. So, try and understand when the face of the agent that sold insurance policy to you changes because you want to opt out before the maturity of your plan.

Some insurance policyholders do not know that the financial upgrade of their agents is dependent on them (the policyholders). If you want your financial advisor to earn well in the company he works, do not terminate but instead pay higher premium and give them referrals that are financially buoyant. That is insurance business.

Demotion may be the result of disciplinary action by the employer or for reasons unrelated to the employee such as a change in the financial circumstances of the business. Under the Fair Work Act 2009 (Cth), a demotion will not constitute a dismissal if it does not involve a 'significant' reduction in the employee's remuneration or duties and the person demoted remains employed with the employer (Lisa More 2015). The same applies in demotion of insurance salespersons. Some agents are demoted due to high rate of termination by their customers and the company still retains them.

8.2 Termination and Loss of Earnings

That is another reason why an agent will not be happy to see you terminate the policy you have been running for years. Please leave this policy to run till maturity is what you usually hear from them at this point.

They know that you terminating will reduce their earnings. It will reduce their take home at the end of the month.

Nobody likes shortage. Even you as a reader of this book like full-time benefit. So, the agent will still like to have full-time earning from the service he sold to you at the end of the month.

So, understand the angle the young man comes from when he tries to convince you to allow your policy to continue to be in force when you come for termination. The young man wants to grow his money. He has some bills to pay and because of that will not allow you do what will affect his commission.

He might have planned what he will use the commission to come to do and you want to reduce it by terminating your contract. Maybe he gets $80,000 as commission in most months and he is expecting the commission to be $90,000 by next month as a result of newly closed businesses that will result to the increase. And the commission he gets from your policy whenever you pay your premium is $2,000. The termination of your policy which implies you stop paying premiums will make the commission short $2,000. That is to say that the agent receives $88,000 instead of the expected $90,000 by next month.

Low earning which can result from customers polices termination has frustrated many agents out of insurance business. But nevertheless, if you as a policyholder want to terminate your policy irrespective of the fact that the agent is preventing you from doing that, you can still terminate.

The solution may be you calling head office of the insurance company and then terminate your policy. The premium paid is yours so you have every right to terminate your policy when you like.

But keep in mind that if the policy you want to terminate is a long term endowment policy, you may get charged depending on how long you have saved so far. If the policy is less than one year of being in force, you may not be able to terminate but all depends on the design of the policy by the company.

8.3 Unfair Treatment during Termination

Some policyholders are not treated pleasantly during termination of their policies. The customer calls the agent for termination and the agent feels angry. Sometimes the agent refuses to answer the phone calls of his client that wants to terminate his existing policy. The behaviour of this kind is not a good one but it all happens because the salesperson is not happy due to the fact that the customer wants to terminate his policy.

Policyholders are pushed around during the termination of their insurance policies. They visit the nearby office of the insurance company and make their intention known to the unit manager of the branch. The manager responds that he will like to see the agent to the policyholder before going on for the termination. He dismisses the customer to go that he will speak with the agent.

He may give the customer a date for him to come back again so that he may have spoken with the agent. Sometimes the customer comes back at the appointed date but no positive answer from the unit manager on the termination request of her policy. The manager may keep pushing the holder around just to know if he, the policyholder, will continue with the policy and do not terminate it again.

The attitudes of some salespersons change on hearing that their customers want to terminate. These agents were nice to the customers when they were paying their premiums as of when due. But they can become rude all of a sudden when the customer wants to bow out before maturity. They do not want the customer to go. They always want their clients to stay irrespective of anything.

References

- Lisa More (2015), I Have Been Demoted by an Employer. Is this Legal?, published by Legal Vision PTY Ltd, Pyrmont NSW, Australia
- Wikipedia (2019), Demotion, published by Wikipedia, San Francisco, United States

Chapter 9

Term Insurance

It is not all about picking term insurance. It is not all about signing into pure life insurance policy with any life insurance company of your choice because you want to insure your life against death. It is more than that. There are some things you have to understand concerning term insurance. It is not as if term insurance is bad. It is a good insurance plan but the fact is that there are some important things you have to know concerning the plan so that you do not feel bad in the long run.

9.1 What is Term Insurance?

Term insurance is one of the purest forms of insurance that one can ever buy. This is a plan which helps the family provide financial assistance in case of death of the breadwinner of the family. It's one of the cheapest and the most simplest forms of financial coverage that we can provide to the family (Ashish 2019). Term insurance is a type of life insurance that provides financial support to the family of the assured person if the person whose life is insured dies.

Term insurance is one of the oldest forms of insurance plans. In fact, more than 60% of people that have been hearing about insurance know about it than any other kind of insurance. When you tell some persons to buy insurance, the place their minds go to first is on term insurance.

Those who do not like insurance because of bad experience some people have had refuses to hear any other thing you want to say to them once you bring to their notice that you want to sell insurance to them. It has been a problem that many insurance companies have been facing for years now.

In Nigeria for instance, many people do not want to hear anything about insurance. Whether you sell endowment plan or term insurance plan, many of the prospects do not want to hear. That is why the penetration of insurance sales is low in the country. "Nigeria's insurance penetration of 0.4 percent has been described as one of the lowest in Africa. Oni said that the nation's insurance penetration of 0.4 percent figure makes its insurance sector a non-starter compared with South Africa with 16.9 percent and Kenya with 2.9 percent penetration respectively" (Cynthia Alo 2018).

Nigerians believe that insurance do not pay. But sometimes the people they believe their families are not paid in the event of death do not follow the due process. They forget that one the reasons for not paying claim to the beneficiary of the live assured is because the life assured was not paying his or her premium as of when due when he or she was alive.

The judgement of many Nigerians that say insurance companies do not pay death claim is one-sided. People are paid when they practice and adhere to the terms and conditions guiding the policy.

9.2 Who can buy Term Insurance?

Term insurance can be bought by fathers, mothers, or even single and people in any part of the world. Death can occur anytime irrespective of the age of any person. Because of this reason, buying of term insurance can be by any person that shows interest.

Nobody owns his or her life and because of that can buy any term insurance from life insurance Company of his or her choice. It is a personal decision made by people.

The return in buying term insurance is dependent on some factors. The factors are age, duration, gender and premiums as applied in other insurance types.

When insurance companies sell term plan to young people, the calculated return is usually high because the young have less chances of dying than the older. So if a young person buys a term insurance policy and pays same premium with an older person, the beneficiary of the young stands the chance of making higher financial claim in the event of death of the young than the beneficiary of the older policyholder. That is the philosophy of insurance companies and it is true in real life.

Also, gender is another important factor. Women have higher sum assured in term insurance than men. This is because it is believed that female gender has lesser likelihood of dying early than men.

So if two different sexes of same age pick term insurance policy to pay same premium, the beneficiary of the female gender will make higher monetary claim than that of the male in the event of death of the life insured.

Premium and duration matters as well. It implies that the higher the premium, the bigger the claim to be made. Also, the lengthier the term policy duration, the bigger the claim to be paid to the beneficiary if the unforeseen happen. Note that term insurance is the cheapest type of insurance to buy.

9.3 Conditions for making Claim in Term Insurance

There are basic conditions to know while buying term insurance. Your financial advisor may not tell you all these things but they are very important. So, open your eyes well to understand this section.

(1) Paying as of when Due

For your beneficiary to be able to make claim without any stress, make sure you pay your premiums as of when due. Term insurance is cheap but it is delicate at the same time. It is an insurance plan that you have to be very careful with. So make sure you maintain good level of consistency.

Paying up front can be very important so that the insurance company will not have any excuse to give when your beneficiary comes to make claim. Many insurance companies are good at speaking big grammar when it comes to claim due to inconsistency in payment.

You can close their mouths from speaking big grammar to your beneficiary by making sure you make your payment completely when you are alive.

You can place your payment to be automatic. This will make you to be faithful in your payment. With automatic payment, there will be standing order on your account. The bank transfers the money into the insurance company's account number every month automatically.

If the automatic debit fails in any month, walk to the insurance company and make your payment or pay into the bank account of the company with your policy number clearly stated. If the life insured fails to pay for a particular month if the payment frequency is monthly, he will lose the cover. If you agree to be paying yearly at the beginning of the policy, also maintain the same standard. As stated before, term insurance is delicate and you must make sure you keep to what is stated in the contract.

(2) Mindful of the Time Interval for Claim

Something the beneficiary to any term insurance should know is to understand the period stated by the insurance company to come and make claim if the life assured die. This is very important and must be taken into consideration by both the person signing into term insurance policy and the beneficiary. There is always duration stated from the time of the death of the life insured for the beneficiary or the family of the deceased to come and make claim.

In the Family Income Protection Plan (FIPP) of FBN Insurance term plan, the maximum time is 12 months (one year) from the date of death of the life insured. What it means is that the beneficiary must inform the insurance company that insured the life of the policyholder within one year of his death for them to make payment to the beneficiary. The company cannot pay claim to any beneficiary that comes to make claim one year after the death of the policyholder.

Many people have lost the benefits entitled to them because they do not inform the insurer on time. Informing the company on time will make them carry out the necessary investigation before they pay. It is important to know this. So ensure you make enquiry from your agent on the appropriate time your beneficiary can come and make claim if you cease to exist.

(3) Keep your Policy Schedule and Number Safe

Some companies ask for policy schedules during claim making in risk plans or term plans as many know it. But whether some demand for it during claim or not, it is important to keep it safe. This will make your beneficiary to make claim easily if the unforeseen happen.

A policy schedule is a document sent to a policyholder through the agent stating the address of the policyholder, the premium, total yearly contributions to be made and the sum assured of the policyholder.

According to Insuranceopedia, policy schedule is also known as a schedule of insurance. It is the part of the insurance contract that identifies the policyholder and details the property and persons covered, the amount of coverage, the exclusions, the deductibles, and the payment mode and schedule (Insuranceopedia 2019).

Agents are usually instructed to deliver the policy schedules to the individual customers but some do not do that due to their laziness and tight schedule.

But in the recent time, agents that do not deliver policy schedules to their customers are not paid commission on such businesses. Some insurance companies in the recent time attach policy acknowledgement slips to the schedules sent to the customers, once the agent delivers the schedules to the customers, the customers sign the acknowledgement slips, the agent then scans back to the head office. With this, the agent is paid commission on the businesses. You can ask your insurance agent for your own policy schedule if he has not given yours to you. Some insurers take policy schedule serious before they issue payment to the beneficiary.

Also it is important that your beneficiary or family know your policy number. It is through your policy number that an administrator in insurance office tracks the payments you made for your life insurance. Always make your policy number known to your family. It makes claim easy.

References

- Ashish (2019), What is Term Insurance?| What, Why and How?, Finwizard Technology Pvt Ltd., India
- Cynthia Alo (2018),Nigeria ranks low in insurance penetration in Africa – Oni, Published by Vanguard News, Lagos, Nigeria
- Insuranceopedia (2019), Policy Schedule, published by Insuranceopedia Inc., United States

Chapter 10

The Importance of Buying Insurance

You see advertisement of various insurance companies on television channels, newspapers, and online as you read through some articles. Yes they need customers because they are also important. Buying insurance and paying your premiums can help you strike good balance in life. No matter the kind of insurance you have bought or planning to buy, just know that insurance is good. There are many benefits attached to it. You cannot manage your own risk but insurance companies help you do that.

As we grow older, get married, build families and start businesses, we come to realize more and more that life insurance is a fundamental part of having a sound financial plan. Depending on your type of policy, life insurance is fairly cheap, which means there's no excuse not to get coverage now. Plus, over the years, you'll find comfort in knowing money will be available to protect your loved ones in the event of your passing. Here are a few other reasons why having life insurance is important (Pay Off Life 2016).

"For many people, their first experience with life insurance is when a friend or acquaintance gets an insurance license. In my case, a college friend, recently hired by a major insurance company, contacted me (along with all of his other friends) to buy a $10,000 policy underwritten by his company. Unfortunately, however, this is how most people acquire life insurance – they don't buy it, it is sold to them."

But is life insurance something that you truly need, or is it merely an inconvenience shoved under your nose by a salesperson? While it may seem like the latter is true, there are actually many reasons why you should purchase life insurance (Michael Lewis 2017)"

Insurance, of all kinds, is used to help protect consumers when certain things happen. For the most part, this protection comes in the form of money. It can also provide protection from liability, damages, and financial loss, but in the end, it usually comes down to money (Peter Kenny 2007).

The importance of insurance cuts across so many areas of life. In school, health, banking, automobile, marine, businesses, agriculture and so many other areas, the importance of insurance is witnessed. Some families are not experiencing financial burden today because of the many benefits attached to buying insurance.

We are going to address the importance of buying insurance policies by categories. The reason is because the importance of this area of concentration is versed. So, breaking it down will make the reader understand the importance in a better way. So, know the importance of insurance and buy any that suits your need properly.

In the developed or developing countries, insurance sector contributes immensely to economic growth as no nation can survive without insurance as risks are prevalent in every sector of the economy (Lanre Ojuola 2015). Even a small market trader in a community market needs to manage her risk properly. Insurance is good and all sectors that help in piloting the affairs of any country have to buy into it.

10.1 Importance of General Insurance

General insurance as one of the broad classification of insurance is of importance in our society today. The importance of General Insurance are as follow:

1. Car insurance protects the car owner from spending huge amount of money in the unfortunate event of car accident. This saves the car owner the stress of searching for where to borrow money to repair the car. Because the car has insurance cover, the insurance company that covers the car spends the money for the repair of the vehicle.

2. The importance of general insurance is observed in home insurance coverage. Home insurance is a comprehensive policy that covers fire, flooding and burglary. Imagine paying a premium of $2,000 to get cover of more than $11,000 should in case such unforeseen circumstance occurs. Home insurance is important as it saves home owners the stress of breaking bank to build a new one. Insurance is very important and every home owner needs to get covered.

3. The importance of insurance is observed in academic institutions. The schools are insured and this has saved school owners the stress of starting afresh to build new schools. Almost all universities in United States of America are insured and these universities make claim in the event of any unpleasant damages.

4. Business owners are happy because of the insurance that covers their businesses. The importance of insurance is observed in businesses which are protected from burglary, thieft or fire. In the occurrence of any of these unforeseen, the business owner makes claim to continue his or her businesses. Insurance has made many businessmen and women stand tall when people thought that they have lost everything.

5. In case of loss of personal property due to natural calamities or man- made, you will not be worrying too much since general insurance almost covers everything. As long as you had insured your properties, you will receive enough amount of money depending on the agreement and policy that you had agreed upon. In summary, general insurance gives you peace of mind.

10.2 The Importance of Life Insurance

In Africa, many people do not want to hear anything about death. Even the elderly do not want to die because of his or her philosophy about death. But of the truth, everyone will die one day. Because of this ideology, many people in that continent do not want to hear anything about life insurance. Religious believe plays a lot of roles in acceptance of life insurance in Africa.

But the truth remains that an understanding man should understand the importance of life insurance.

Importance of Term Insurance

We will be considering the importance of term insurance which is a part of life insurance types. The importance of term insurance is as follow:

(1) Term insurance gives peace of mind to the family of the life insured. The family do not have to be poor or face financial difficulties in the death of the policyholder or the assured life. This peace of mind can keep them to live similar standard life they were living when the breadwinner of the family was alive.

(2) Some term insurance covers funeral expenses. This makes the family to avoid financial burden that is associated with funeral expenses. In the Igbo tribe of Nigeria for instance, funeral ceremony is an expensive occasion. One who covers his life with good premium payment will have his family spend less at his demise. It acts as a real support for your family, if something happens to the bread earner. This support lasts for long and it motivates the family.

3. It gives sense of security to the beneficiary and the family. Security is the state of being free from danger or threat. When issue arises, the monetary value claimed from life insurance coverage can go a long way.

4. A good Term insurance plan helps you protect yourself even better by covering the bid 3 Ds of your life: Death, Disease and Disability. The importance of term insurance in this regard is that the insured do need to pay to the hospital when he or she faces critical illness. The insurance covers that.

Importance of Endowment Insurance

(1) Endowment insurance plan helps policyholders to spend less and plan more. It makes people to moderate their monthly expenses as they plan their lives better ahead.

(2) It gives a kind of free money to the customers. Imagine having about $500, 000 in five years. And in some cases the money is saved with less stress especially when premium is paid automatically from the bank account of the policyholders.

(3) Endowment products give financial security to the holders. When you have such plan, you are financially secure because you know you have good sum of money somewhere. The only thing is that you cannot access the money at that point in time.

(4) It put smile on the face of civil servants. Maybe a civil servant is retiring from work in ten years from today and picks an endowment plan to save for ten years. If he saves good premium monthly, he can have enough to even build new house at retirement.

(5) Education endowment plans save parents the stress of school fees when the children are of age of gaining admission into higher institutions. The money saved for the children over the years can go a long way in keeping them going in schools.

(6) Another importance of education endowment plan is in education security. What it implies is that it guarantees the education of the child. If the policyholder (the parent in most cases) dies during the savings, the education of the child is secured. The insurance company pays some percentage of the assured sum to the guardian of the child up till the university level. But it depends on the policy term of the particular insurance company.

(7) The plan helps customers meet family demand in future. Take for instance that a customer picks the plan when he was single and then got married when the policy approaches maturity, the paid money when the policy finally matures can be enough to start a business for the new wife. Also, the claim can take care of other family demand. Endowment plans have a lot of importance.

10.3 The Importance of Insurance to Nations

People may not believe the statistics on the profits insurance companies have made over the years or on yearly basis. United States of America where insurance sells much cannot deny that insurance has not contributed in one way or the other towards the growth of the country.

The World Insurance Report has shown that insurance companies wrote US$2,443.7 billion in premium worldwide in 2000. Of the total, US$ 15,221.3 billion, i.e 63% was generated by life business while US$ 922.4, i.e about 45% was generated by non-life business, translating into a 9.1% increase in Life Insurance and 2.7% in non-life insurance over 1999 figure when adjusted for inflation (Dr. Olusanya Oba 2003).

U.S. insurance industry net premiums written totalled $1.2 trillion in 2017, with premiums recorded by life/health (L/H) insurers accounting for 52 percent, and premiums by property/casualty (P/C) insurers accounting for 48 percent, according to S&P Global Market Intelligence. The country has high insurance penetration and makes profit.

Also, Insurance companies in EU/EEA countries collected gross premiums worth USD 1.2 trillion in 2016, representing 28% of premiums collected by insurance countries in all participating countries (Organisation for Economic Co-operation and Development 2018).

With all these statistics, it is clear that insurance industry has contributed hugely to every nation. We will now give step by step points on the importance of insurance to nations. The importance of insurance to nations/countries is as follow:

(1) Insurance improves and supports the economy of the member countries. Insurance companies have invested a lot of money in real estate, bonds and other areas. This helps in national growth and economic development of nations in all.

(2) Insurance helps in job creation. They have help to reduce the unemployment rate of many countries globally. Insurance have employed many people in so many countries and they pay their workers to meet their daily needs. FBN Insurance for example which has been into life insurance for just 8 years has over 3,000 employed salespersons nationwide as of the year 2019.

(3) Insurance helps in managing of countries risk. No country is free from perils. Because of this, insurance works to protect the citizens in case any of the unforeseen circumstances happen. Take for example that there is fire outbreak in the oil industry of a country and the industry is insured. Insurance will help the company bounce back and gain ground fast as claim is paid.

References

- AXA Mansard (2015), Home Insurance, published by AXA Mansard Insurance PLC, Victoria Island, Lagos, Nigeria
- HDFCLife (2018), Term Insurance and why it is important for everybody, published by HDFC Life Insurance Company Limited, Mumbai, India
- Lanre Ojuola (2015), Insurance as a Tool for Sustainable Growth, published by Chattered Insurance Institute of Nigeria Journal, ISSN 117-9031, Vol 15, No 1, April 2015
- Michael Lewis (2012), 6 Reasons Why You Should Buy Life Insurance, published by Spark Charge Media, LLC., Texas, United States
- OECD (2018), Global Insurance Market Trends, published by Organisation for Economic Co-operation and Development, Paris, France
- Pay Off Life (2016), 5 Important Reasons Why You Need Life Insurance, Published by Pay Off Life Insurance, Costa Mesa, California, United States
- Peter Kenny (2007), Why is Insurance Important?, published by Streetdirectory Pte Ltd, Paya Lebar Square, Singapore
- The Cheaper Insurance (2015), The Importance of General Insurance, published by The Cheaper Insurance, United States

Chapter 11

Claim Making

This is the last chapter of the book and it appears on the right section. The essence of buying insurance is to get coverage or protection and that protection comes when the policyholder or the beneficiary makes claim. When you make claim without less stress and paid early as it suppose to be, your mind is filled with joy at the end.

When you make a claim on an insurance policy, you are formally notifying the insurance company that you have suffered a loss or damage that you believe is covered by the policy and you are requesting action. The insurer will review your claim and see if the event or circumstances are risks covered by the policy. You will need to provide proof it is a genuine claim and the insurer will need to be certain the claim satisfies the terms and conditions of your insurance policy (Insurance Council of Australia 2013)

Every insurance company has steps to come for claim when damages occur or when your policy matures. Do well to ask your financial advisor or insurance broker to be able to make claim as fast as possible when the need comes. Sometimes when it comes to endowment plans, term insurance, and general businesses, there are specific items or documents needed before claim is successfully made. Also, requirements are dependent on country and the insurance company but we will do well to cover as many areas as possible in this chapter.

According to Marie Curie on claim making he stated, "Let the insurer know you plan to make a claim. The quickest way to do this is by phone. The number should be in the policy documents or you can find it online. You can also contact the insurer by email or post. They will tell you what you need to do to claim" (Marie Curie 2018).

11.1 Insurance Companies pay Claim

Many people believe that insurance companies do not pay claim. This has been in the mind of so many people over the years. Because of this, many people are afraid of buying insurance because they still believe that risk management companies do not pay claim. But, their philosophy is wrong. The author as a financial advisor has seen many policyholders and beneficiaries come for their claim benefits and they get paid.

So it is time for change of philosophy. Do not discourage any person from buying insurance service from any registered company that is permitted to sell insurance. You philosophy may be wrong. Do not think that you know it all about insurance claim.

So, change your thinking and how you see insurance companies. They pay claim, no doubt. So avoid any act of discouraging anyone from buying insurance. If any person told you that a particular insurance company did not pay him claim or someone he knows. Ask him properly or take a step to the insurance company and make enquiry. There may be something he did not do well that made the company deny him or her, his or her claim benefits. Maybe there was breach of contract but the individual did not tell you.

11.2 Facts on Claims Paid by Insurance Industry

Facts and figures have shown that insurance companies pay claim. In India, Nigeria, Australia, United States of America, Canada and the other parts of the world, insurance companies pay claims when they are due. So, do not be afraid of buying insurance because of the rumour that companies that sell insurance do not pay.

Life insurance benefits and claims totalled $697 billion in 2017. This includes life insurance death benefits, annuity benefits, disability benefits and other payouts, and compares with $670 billion in 2016. The largest payout, $309 billion, was for surrender benefits and withdrawals from life insurance contracts made to policyholders who terminated their policies early or withdrew cash from their policies - NAIC data, sourced from Insurance Information Institute

Australia

General Insurers pay out an average of $135.9 million in claims to policyholders each working day. They only decline 3.6% of claims*. In 2017-18, insurers approved 3,361,016 claims from policyholders.

About 6.9 per cent of home and contents policyholders and 15.7 per cent of motor vehicle policyholders lodged claims in the December quarter of 2018 - Code Governance Committee General Insurance in Australia Report (2016-17), p.20, Table 8

Nigerian

Cornerstone Insurance PLC said it paid gross claims of N4.5 billion to claimants in its 2016 financial year, representing an increase of 61 per cent from the N2.8 billion posted the previous year. At the 2016 Annual General Meeting(AGM) of the Consolidated Hallmark Insurance Plc in Lagos, its chairman, Mr. Obinna Ekezie, said the company recorded growth in claims payment as it rose from N1.34 billion in 2015 to N1.73 billion in 2016, representing an increase of 29 per cent. Rock Insurance Plc paid out N1.45 billion claims in 2016. For Mutual Benefits Assurance PLC, Ellen Offo said in 2016, the insurer paid out claims amounting to N3.3 billion, which is a 43 per cent increase from the N2.3 billion paid out in 2015 - Source: Leadership News Company of Nigeria.

United Kingdom

According to data from Insurance Europe, in 2017, insurance companies in United Kingdom paid total claim benefits of €224050 million to policyholders and beneficiaries. This includes claims from life benefits, health claims and non-life claims, breakdowns by motor, property and accident.

Spain

In the same year 2017, insurance industry in Spain paid claims totalled €26639 million to her customers. This is sourced from Insurance Europe as well.

United States

Hurricane Ike hit America in September 2008, grinding North America's infrastructure to a halt and demolishing prime agriculture, buildings and causing flooding across the lands of Cuba, Texas and Haiti amongst other areas. Ike cause 195 deaths either indirectly or directly; 113 of which were in the United States. The damage caused saw 131,000 insurance claims filed in the first few days of the storm in Ohio alone, with an estimate of over $553 million to have been paid out to that state. In Texas, 44,000 flood and 800,000 windstorm claims were submitted costing up to nearly $12 billion - Ashburnham Insurance Services Limited. Nearly $133 Billion was paid as claim for auto insurance in United States of America in 2014 (Jeff Ryan 2016).

With all these facts and figures, it is believed that insurance companies pay claim. So, feel free to buy insurance.

11.3 You are paid at the due Date

Insurance are happy paying her customers at the due date. The due date as implies here means the maturity time. It is not paying you as a result of you surrendering your policy because of one challenge or the other. If you are buying an endowment policy from any insurance company, be patient till the maturity so that you can have your cash benefits and the other accrued benefits attached to it.

It is not all about what the agent told you but about what is stated in the policy documents or terms and conditions. An agent may tell you that a particular endowment insurance plan matures in 3 years while it is a five years plan.

So check the proposal form properly to understand the real maturity time to make your claim without any much quarrel with anyone. Paying your premium at the due date guarantees your claim payout.

The same thing applies for term insurance as well. In term insurance, the beneficiary gets paid at the death of the life insured. So any beneficiary that wants to make claim should inform the life insured to keep to what is stated in the policy statement. The same applies in general insurance policies. If there are damages and the insurance policy covers that, the policyholder is paid claim for that.

11.4 Go for Your Claim at the Right Time

If you know when your policy has reached its maturity, go for your claim benefits. Do not wait for any insurance company to call you telling you that your policy has mature and therefore you should come and make claim. Many insurance companies do not have time for that. In fact, many will not want you to come for your claim exactly the time of your policy maturity because they will like to do more businesses with the fund you saved with them.

When you enter into any endowment policy with any insurance company, take note of the date it starts and the date it will mature. You can write it down in your diary so that you do not forget. Also, you can create a reminder using your phone so that you do not forget. Any way you want to do it, just go on with it. The fact is that you should keep record so that you do not forget or lose sight of your policy maturity date.

If your father bought term insurance (pure life insurance policy) and use you as the beneficiary, make sure you inform the insurance company immediately your father dies and the policy is still in force. This will make the insurance company to come and investigate the date and also tell you the things you will get to make your claim easily. Do not wait until the funeral is over. You may not have the facts the insurance company may need after the funeral. So, immediately the death occurs, do well to go to the insurance office which your father bought the life cover from and inform them. You can also call your father's insurance agent if you have his contact and inform him.

Some insurance companies have time limit which you can report the death of the life insured. After this period, the beneficiary cannot make a death claim. Example is one year grace time for report in FBN Insurance.

Insurance sometimes do not go in line with the culture of a particular community or ethnic group. Example is in some ethnic groups in Africa. In Igbo land of Nigeria for example, a woman whose husband is dead is not allowed to go out until the burial of the husband is carried out and after the burial is also conditioned by the culture to stay for some months in the house. The total duration for all these time of mourning can be up to 6 months. That means if the woman happens to be the beneficiary of the husband's life insurance policy, she is not allowed to visit the insurer to report the case of the death of the husband.

In respect to this scenario, if the time stated that the beneficiary should report from the time of death of the life insured is 6 months, the woman losses the benefit because of the culture of the land. Insurance is insurance and not a sector for observing traditions and culture of any particular community. In respect to that, some cultures need to be broken for women to claim the life benefits of their husbands. Wisdom is profitable to direct and because of that women should go for the claim entitled to them irrespective of any old culture of the family. Because of civilization, most of these irrational cultures are becoming weak in Africa.

11.5 Requirements to make Claim

In this section, we will be discussing requirements to make claim from any insurance company. It is an important section and you have to know them.

Making claim for Term or Whole Life Policies

There are basic requirements to make claim for term or whole life policies. These requirements are as follow:

(1) The policy must be active

(2) The terms and conditions of the policy must apply

(3) The policy schedule sent by the company to you either through your agent or directly to you

(4) A filled in claim form. It can be done electronically or manually

(5) The original or a certified copy of the medical certificate of cause of death or other proof of death satisfactory to the company

(6) Proof to the satisfaction of the company of the age of the life assured, if not previously provided at the commencement of the policy

(7) The original or certified copies of the identity documents, passports or other satisfactory evidence of identity of the deceased and the person who is claiming the benefit

(8) Proof of bank account number and branch code should the claimant wish the benefits to paid directly into their bank account

(9) A police report providing accidental death, if the death of the life insured was not from natural causes

(10) Any other documents/reports, which the company deems necessary to assess the claim

(11) In some insurance companies, you must submit a death claim with all documents within one year of the death of the person covered under the policy. If you make the death claim more than a year after the death, the company will not pay the benefit.

Note: If the company rejects a claim, the claim will not be paid. You then can challenge the rejected claim to court if you feel cheated or not treated well. If the life insured owe the company missed premiums, the amount that you owe will be deducted from the money you receive for the claim provided the policy has not lapsed.

Requirements to make Claim for Endowment Plans

There are requirements for claim making in every kind of insurance plan. The requirements for investment plans are not same with that of term plans. Life and death are far from each other.

The basic requirements to make claim in endowment policy at its maturity are as follow:

(1) Policy schedule

(2) A well filled claim form

(3) Account details of the policyholder for payment of the maturity benefit into the bank account.

(4) The policy number of the policyholder

(5) The policy must have acquired a cash value

(6) It must be active

(7) The original or a certified copy of the policyholder's 'proof of identity'

For endowment policy whereby the policyholder dies before maturity, the following is needed to make claim:

(1) A completed claim form

(2) A medical certificate of cause of death

(3) Proof that the policyholder and deceased are the same person.

Note: Some insurance companies overlook many things when it comes to claim of cash benefits in endowment policy. They ask you of your policy number and your account details and the money you have saved plus the interest get paid into your bank account in eight business days.

Requirements to make Claim for Burglary Insurance (General Insurance)

(1) Notify the company when you notice that some of your valuables have been stolen

(2) File a police report as soon as you discover that you have been robbed.

(3) Call your insurance agent or the insurance company that covers your values to report the incident

(4) Take pictures of the broken parts of your home if any

(5) Gather any receipts you have for the valuables that were stolen

(6) Fill a claim form and make photocopy of it to have your own copy

(7) Submit the claim form to the insurance company

(8) Call the insurance company after a few week to know how far they have gone with the claim you filled.

Note: Some insurance companies may require you to provide other documents not stated here for them

How to make Claim in Fire Insurance

(1) Contact police and get fire incident report from them

(2) Contact the insurance company immediately after that

(3) Snap and store the picture of the fire incidence

(4) Calculate the estimate of the worth of goods or valuables destroyed by the fire

(5) Fill claim form before or after the insurer sends their staff to investigate the damages

(6) Check on the insurance company frequently to receive your financial claim benefit.

References

- Amber Keefer (2012), How to Make the Best Theft Insurance Claim, published by The Nest, New York, United States
- FBN Insurance, Extended Family Support Plan, published by FBN Insurance, Lagos state, Nigeria
- Insurance Council of Australia (2013), Claims explained, published by Insurance Council of Australia, Australia
- Jeff Ryan (2016), How much do auto insurers in the USA pay out each year in claims?, published by Quora, California, United States of America
- Marie Curie (2018), Claiming on Someone's life Insurance after they've died, published by Marie Curie Registered Charity, London, United Kingdom
- Insurance Europe (2018), Insurance Data, published by Insurance Europe aisbl, Brussels, Belgium
- Steve Smith (2017), 10 Biggest Insurance Claim Payouts of ALL TIME, published by Ashburnham Insurance Services Limited, Southend-on-Sea, Essex, England
- Zaka Khaliq (2017), 10 Insurance Firms Pay N33bn Claims To Nigerians, published by Leadership Newspaper Company, Lagos State, Nigeria

Other Books by the Author
- Choosing and Working as an Insurance Agent
- Guide to Youth Challenges
- Basic Information in Youth and Youth Empowerment
- Importance of Youth Empowerment
- Types of Youth Empowerment
- Metallurgical and Materials Engineering: Introduction and Applications
- Powder Metallurgy: Its Engineering Consideration and Applications on Copper
- Nigerian Youth Challenges
- Young Fraudsters in Nigeria (Yahoo or G Boys)

www.ingramcontent.com/pod-product-compliance
Lightning Source LLC
Chambersburg PA
CBHW021834170526
45157CB00007B/2798